ANNA WILSON

2023 TRAVEL GUIDE TO ATLANTA

The Ultimate Guide to Explore the Hidden Gems of The Dream City,Must see Attractions and Adventures

First edition

Contents

Introduction

Welcome to the ultimate travel guide for your road trip to Atlanta! In this book, "Travel Guide Road Trip to Atlanta Embark on an Unforgettable Road Trip to Atlanta's Hidden Gems"we invite you to embark on an extraordinary journey filled with exploration, adventure, and discovery.

Atlanta, the bustling capital of Georgia, is a city teeming with rich history, diverse cultures, and captivating sights waiting to be unveiled. Whether you're a seasoned road-tripper or a first-time adventurer, this guide is tailored to enhance your experience and ensure you make the most of your time in this vibrant metropolis.

Beyond its well-known attractions like the Georgia Aquarium, World of Coca-Cola, and Centennial Olympic Park, Atlanta has a treasure trove of hidden wonders waiting to be discovered. From quaint neighborhoods brimming with character to charming boutiques and galleries, each corner of the city has something unique to offer. It's these little-known gems that make the journey truly special.

Our aim is to take you beyond the well-trodden paths and introduce you to Atlanta's best-kept secrets, those hidden gems that only the locals know about. From scenic drives that immerse you in the beauty of nature to offbeat attractions that spark curiosity and wonder, we have meticulously curated an itinerary that promises unforgettable moments and lasting memories.

Through these pages, you will find detailed insights into planning your road trip, selecting the perfect route, and discovering the must-see landmarks that define the essence of Atlanta. Moreover, we'll guide you towards lesser-known spots that reveal the true heart and soul of the city, allowing you to connect with its authentic culture and traditions.

As you traverse through Atlanta's diverse landscapes, you'll encounter a tapestry of cultures, each contributing to the city's vibrant identity. Engage with the locals, strike up conversations with fellow travelers, and let the stories you gather along the way enrich your experience.

Amidst the excitement and wonder, we also provide practical advice to ensure a smooth and safe voyage. From packing smartly to navigating unfamiliar roads, we've got you covered with valuable tips that will make your road trip stress-free and enjoyable.

As you venture on this road trip, we encourage you to embrace spontaneity, engage with fellow travelers, and create your unique stories to share with friends and family. Our journey doesn't end with mere sightseeing; it extends to experiencing the local art, music, and culinary delights that contribute to Atlanta's vibrant tapestry.

So fasten your seatbelts, grab your map, and prepare to be enchanted by the charm of Atlanta's hidden treasures. Let this guide be your trusted companion as you navigate through the city's winding roads and uncover the true essence of Atlanta on an unforgettable road trip like no other. Get ready to embark on an adventure that will leave you inspired, amazed, and longing for more.

Remember, the essence of any road trip lies not only in the destinations you reach but also in the moments between them. Embrace the unexpected detours, relish in the mesmerizing landscapes, and take a moment to appreciate the small wonders that present themselves along the way.

So, get ready to embark on a remarkable road trip to Atlanta's hidden treasures. This book is your ticket to an unforgettable adventure filled with unforgettable memories. Let the excitement build as you turn the page and delve into the heart of Atlanta, where remarkable experiences await at every turn.

Bon voyage, and may your road trip to Atlanta be a journey of a lifetime!

Hello Atlanta

Welcome to Atlanta, in this ultimate travel guide for your road trip to Atlanta! In this chapter, we will set the stage for your thrilling adventure and provide essential insights to help you make the most of your journey. From an overview of Atlanta's allure to the significance of embarking on a road trip, this comprehensive introduction will prepare you to explore the hidden gems of this captivating city.

1.1 About Atlanta

Nestled in the heart of Georgia, Atlanta stands as a vibrant and dynamic metropolis, boasting a rich history and a blend of diverse cultures. From its roots as a transportation hub during the Civil War to its pivotal role in the civil rights movement, Atlanta has played a crucial part in shaping the nation's history. Today, it is a bustling city that embraces progress while cherishing its heritage.

Atlanta, a city with a captivating past and a forward-thinking spirit, beckons travelers from all corners of the world. Founded in 1837 as the final terminus of a railroad line, the city quickly burgeoned into a vital transportation hub, earning the nickname "The Gate City." Today, Atlanta's status as a major metropolis continues to thrive, making it a must-visit destination for travelers seeking a blend of history, culture, and contemporary allure.

History enthusiasts will find Atlanta's heritage enthralling. As you explore the city, you'll encounter various landmarks that tell the story of its evolution, from the antebellum architecture of the Oakland Cemetery to the storied halls of the Martin Luther King Jr. National Historical Park. Visit the Atlanta History Center to immerse yourself in exhibits that trace the city's growth, or stroll through the restored district of Sweet Auburn, where Dr. King's legacy is celebrated.

However, Atlanta is not just a city living in the past. It has embraced modernity with open arms, becoming a global city renowned for its business prowess, technological innovations, and vibrant arts scene. The skyline is punctuated by contemporary architectural marvels, such as the iconic Bank of America Plaza and the gleaming glass facades of Midtown's skyscrapers. The city's commitment to the arts is evident in the High Museum of Art, a beacon of culture featuring an impressive collection of European and American art.

Moreover, Atlanta's passion for sports and entertainment is palpable. Catch a thrilling Atlanta Braves baseball game at Truist Park or witness electrifying basketball matches with the Atlanta Hawks. The city's numerous entertainment venues host concerts, theater performances, and major events that cater to diverse tastes, making sure there's always something happening in the vibrant heart of Atlanta.

Atlanta's vibrant neighborhoods add a layer of diversity and charm to its allure. From the trendy streets of Buckhead to the artistic vibe of Little Five Points, each district offers a unique flavor and a trove of hidden gems waiting to be explored. Discover quirky boutiques, delectable eateries, and thriving nightlife scenes that will leave an indelible impression on your journey.

This travel guide will lead you through Atlanta's multifaceted landscape, revealing the city's intriguing past, vibrant present, and promising future. Whether you're a history buff, a culture enthusiast, or an adventurer seeking new experiences, Atlanta promises to delight and captivate you at every turn.

1.2 Why Choose a Road Trip to Atlanta?

A road trip offers an unparalleled sense of freedom and adventure, allowing you to connect with the journey as much as the destination. Unlike other forms of travel, a road trip empowers you to dictate your pace, take spontaneous detours, and explore off-the-beaten-path wonders that often remain hidden from conventional tourists.

Embarking on a road trip to Atlanta offers a unique and enriching travel experience that goes beyond the typical tourist destinations. The allure of hitting the open road, the freedom to choose your route, and the flexibility to explore at your own pace, why a road trip is the ideal way to discover the hidden gems of this fascinating city are:

- Flexibility and Freedom:

One of the primary advantages of a road trip is the unparalleled sense of freedom it offers. Unlike other modes of travel, you have the liberty to modify your itinerary on the go. Feel drawn to a scenic detour? No problem - simply change your route and follow the allure of the unknown. With the open road stretching before you, every mile is a canvas upon which you can paint your own adventure.

- Immersive Experience:

A road trip allows you to become fully immersed in the destinations you visit. You're not just passing through; you're actively engaging with the landscapes, cultures, and communities along the way. You'll have the opportunity to meet locals, discover offbeat attractions, and connect with the essence of each place you encounter. This immersion enriches your understanding of Atlanta and creates lasting memories.

• Hidden Gems and Local Discoveries:

While popular tourist spots are undoubtedly worth exploring, a road trip opens the door to hidden gems that often remain undiscovered by conventional travelers. As you venture away from the beaten path, you'll stumble upon charming small towns, scenic byways, and locally beloved attractions that reveal the soul of Atlanta. These authentic experiences create a deep connection with the city and its people.

• Spontaneity and Adventure:

There's a thrill in embracing spontaneity on a road trip. Serendipitous encounters, impromptu roadside stops, and unplanned adventures become a part of your journey. It's in these unscripted moments that you'll find unexpected treasures and create stories worth sharing for years to come.

• Bonding and Camaraderie:

If you're traveling with friends or family, a road trip fosters strong bonds and lasting memories. Sharing the excitement of discovery, navigating together, and reveling in the journey create an unbreakable camaraderie. It's not just about reaching the destination; it's about the laughter, conversations, and shared experiences that make the road trip a journey of connection and togetherness.

• Scenic Drives and Natural Beauty:

The road trip to Atlanta offers picturesque drives through breathtaking landscapes. From the rolling hills of the Appalachian Mountains to the verdant beauty of Georgia's countryside, each mile is a canvas of nature's splendor. These scenic drives add an extra dimension of joy to your journey, making the trip as remarkable as the destination itself.

- A Journey of Self-Discovery:

A road trip is not just an exploration of a new city; it's also an opportunity for self-discovery. The solitude and introspection offered by the open road allow you to contemplate, reflect, and gain insights into your own life. It's a chance to find solace in the present moment and rediscover yourself amidst the adventure.

A road trip to Atlanta is much more than a means of transportation; it's a transformative experience that will leave an indelible mark on your heart and soul. Embrace the freedom, the spontaneity, and the joy of the journey as you set forth to discover the hidden treasures of Atlanta. Your road trip awaits, promising unforgettable moments and a deeper connection with this vibrant city and its welcoming spirit. So, get ready to hit the road and let Atlanta's hidden gems unveil themselves before you, one mile at a time.

1.3 Planning Your Adventure

Before setting out on your road trip, thorough planning is essential to ensure a smooth and enjoyable journey. Consider the duration of your trip, the best time to visit Atlanta, and the activities that pique your interest. Create a checklist of essentials to pack, and make sure your vehicle is in top-notch condition for the drive ahead. Familiarize yourself with the different routes to Atlanta, each offering unique scenic views and attractions along the way.

Proper planning is the key to a successful and enjoyable road trip to Atlanta.

From choosing the best time to visit to mapping out your route and ensuring you have all the essentials, thoughtful preparation will set the stage for an unforgettable journey. In this section, we'll walk you through the crucial steps of planning your adventure to make the most of your road trip experience by:

- Determine the Duration:

The first step in planning your road trip is deciding how much time you can dedicate to the journey. Consider your schedule, commitments, and the number of days you can comfortably spare for the trip. Atlanta has a plethora of attractions and hidden gems to explore, so the more time you have, the deeper your immersion into the city's culture and sights will be.

- Best Time to Visit Atlanta:

Before setting your travel dates, research the best time to visit Atlanta. The city experiences a temperate climate, but each season offers a unique charm. Spring (March to May) brings mild weather and blooming flora, making it an ideal time for outdoor exploration. Summer (June to August) offers longer daylight hours and a plethora of festivals and events. Fall (September to November) welcomes pleasant temperatures and vibrant foliage, while winter (December to February) is a quieter season with fewer crowds.

- Create an Itinerary:

Plan a rough itinerary for your road trip, outlining the cities or landmarks you wish to visit and the experiences you want to have along the way. While spontaneity is part of the allure of a road trip, a basic framework will help you stay on track and ensure you don't miss out on must-see attractions.

- Choosing the Route.

Atlanta is accessible from various directions, offering a range of scenic routes and detours. Research different routes and choose the one that aligns with your preferences and interests. The Southern route may take you through charming towns, while the Eastern route offers scenic views of the Appalachian Mountains. Whichever route you choose, ensure it complements the experiences you want to have on your road trip.

- Packing Essentials:

Packing smartly is essential for a comfortable and stress-free road trip. Make a checklist of essential items such as clothing suitable for the weather, toiletries, medications, and any specific gear you might need for planned activities. Don't forget your camera to capture the beautiful moments along the way, and pack a road trip playlist to keep the journey upbeat and enjoyable.

- Vehicle Maintenance:

Before hitting the road, ensure your vehicle is in excellent condition for the journey. Schedule a thorough inspection, including checking the engine, brakes, tires, and fluid levels. Carry a spare tire, jack, and emergency kit in case of unexpected situations. Regular maintenance will not only ensure a smooth journey but also add to your safety on the road.

- Accommodations:

Decide whether you'll be staying at hotels, motels, campgrounds, or a mix of accommodation types. Make advance reservations, especially during peak travel seasons, to secure the best places to stay along your route. If you prefer a more spontaneous approach, consider using camping apps or travel apps that help you find available accommodations on the go.

- Roadside Attractions and Stops:

Part of the fun of a road trip is exploring the quirky and unique roadside attractions and small towns that you encounter along the way. Research interesting stops or landmarks to visit, and don't hesitate to take impromptu detours if something catches your eye. These spontaneous moments often lead to some of the most cherished memories.

- Budgeting Your Road Trip:

Estimate the costs for fuel, accommodation, food, and activities to create a budget for your road trip. Be prepared for unexpected expenses and include a buffer in your budget. It's a good idea to have some cash on hand for places that may not accept card payments, especially in rural areas.

- Staying Connected on the Go:

Ensure you have a reliable means of communication throughout your road trip. Check your phone's network coverage along your route, and consider investing in a portable Wi-Fi hotspot if you'll be relying heavily on navigation apps and staying connected during your journey.

- Helpful Apps and Websites:

Make use of various travel apps and websites to enhance your road trip experience. Navigation apps like Google Maps or Waze will help you find the best routes and avoid traffic, while travel apps like TripAdvisor or Yelp can guide you to local restaurants and attractions with positive reviews.

Preparing for the Journey

Before setting out on your road trip to Atlanta, thorough preparation is essential to ensure a smooth and enjoyable adventure. This chapter delves into the crucial aspects of getting ready for the journey, covering everything from packing essentials and vehicle maintenance to safety precautions. By taking these steps, you can maximize your comfort, safety, and overall road trip experience.

2.1 Packing Essentials

Packing efficiently for your road trip is essential to ensure you have everything you need while avoiding unnecessary clutter.Here's a comprehensive list of packing essentials to ensure you have everything you need for a comfortable and memorable journey:

- Versatile Clothing:

Opt for clothing that can be mixed and matched to create different outfits. This approach allows you to pack light while still having options for various weather conditions and activities. Choose neutral colors and versatile pieces that can be dressed up or down as needed.

- Seasonal Attire:

Check the weather forecast for Atlanta and the regions you'll be traveling through. Pack accordingly, taking into account seasonal variations and potential temperature fluctuations. Layering is especially useful, as it allows you to adapt to changing weather conditions easily.

- Pack for Comfort:

Comfortable clothing and footwear are paramount for a road trip. You'll likely spend hours in the car, exploring, and walking, so prioritize comfort over fashion. Pack supportive and well-cushioned shoes suitable for walking, as well as cozy clothes for relaxing during rest stops or evenings.

- Reusable Containers and Bags:

Bring reusable containers and bags for snacks and food storage. They not only help reduce waste but also keep your snacks organized and fresh. Additionally, having a few reusable shopping bags can be convenient for impromptu shopping or picnics.

- Laundry Solutions:

Pack a small bottle of travel-sized laundry detergent or laundry pods, especially if you plan to be on the road for an extended period. Hand-washing some clothes during your journey can help you refresh your wardrobe and reduce the number of items you need to pack.

- Personal Care and Toiletries:

Consider using travel-sized toiletries to save space and weight. Many stores offer travel-sized versions of common products, such as shampoo, conditioner, body wash, and lotion. You can also transfer essential liquids into reusable travel bottles to minimize waste and stay within TSA liquid restrictions if flying to your starting point.

- Road Trip Snacks:

Having a variety of road trip snacks on hand will keep you energized and help you avoid frequent stops. Pack a mix of healthy options like granola bars, trail mix, and fresh fruits, as well as indulgent treats for occasional splurges.

- Hydration:

Stay well-hydrated throughout your road trip by carrying reusable water bottles. Dehydration can lead to fatigue and decreased alertness, which can be dangerous during long drives. Ensure you have access to plenty of water to stay refreshed and focused.

- Travel Documents:

Keep all your essential travel documents organized in a secure folder or travel wallet. This includes your driver's license, vehicle registration, insurance documents, hotel reservations, attraction tickets, and any other relevant information you may need along the way.

- Emergency Kit:

Pack a comprehensive emergency kit to be prepared for unforeseen situations.

The kit should include items such as a flashlight, batteries, a multi-tool, duct tape, a first-aid kit, a fire extinguisher, and basic repair supplies.

- Personal Entertainment:

Apart from your road trip playlist and audiobooks, consider bringing personal entertainment like books, magazines, or a portable gaming device to keep you occupied during downtime or rest stops.

By thoughtfully curating your packing list and prioritizing comfort, organization, and efficiency, you'll be well-prepared for your road trip to Atlanta. Streamlining your belongings and being mindful of the essentials will not only make packing a breeze but also enhance your overall road trip experience. With your bags packed and your excitement building, you're ready to set off on a remarkable journey to discover the hidden gems of Atlanta.

2.2 Vehicle Maintenance Tips

Ensuring that your vehicle is in excellent condition is paramount for a safe and worry-free road trip. Before setting off on your journey to Atlanta, take the following vehicle maintenance tips into consideration:

- Pre-Trip Inspection:

Schedule a comprehensive pre-trip inspection with a qualified mechanic. This inspection should cover all critical components of your vehicle, including the engine, transmission, brakes, tires, suspension, steering, and exhaust system. Identifying and addressing potential issues before your trip will prevent breakdowns and avoidable delays on the road.

- Fluid Levels:

Check and top up all essential fluids in your vehicle. These include engine oil, transmission fluid, brake fluid, coolant, and windshield washer fluid. Low or dirty fluids can compromise the performance of your car, so it's crucial to maintain them at optimal levels for a smooth and efficient journey.

- Tire Care:

Your tires are the only point of contact between your vehicle and the road, making them vital for safe driving. Check the tire pressure using a reliable gauge and adjust it to the recommended levels specified in your vehicle's owner's manual. Also, inspect the tire tread depth to ensure it meets safety standards. Bald or worn-out tires can lead to reduced traction and handling, especially in adverse weather conditions.

- Spare Tire and Tools:

Confirm that your vehicle's spare tire is in good condition and properly inflated. Additionally, ensure you have the necessary tools to change a tire, including a jack and lug wrench. Familiarize yourself with the tire-changing process before your trip, as it may come in handy in case of a flat tire.

- Battery Check:

A fully functional battery is essential for starting your vehicle and powering its electrical components. Test your battery's charge and voltage to ensure it is in good working condition. Consider having your battery checked by a professional if it's approaching the end of its expected lifespan, Carry jumper cables to help jump-start the vehicle if needed.

- Lights and Signals:

Inspect all exterior lights on your vehicle, including headlights, taillights, brake lights, turn signals, and hazard lights. Replace any burnt-out bulbs before your road trip to ensure optimal visibility and safety, especially during nighttime driving or adverse weather conditions.

- Brake System:

Brakes are a critical safety component of your vehicle. Have your brake system checked by a qualified mechanic to ensure all components are functioning correctly. Squealing or grinding noises, a spongy brake pedal, or vibrations when braking could indicate potential issues that need immediate attention.

- Air Conditioning and Heating:

A comfortable climate inside the vehicle enhances your road trip experience. Ensure your air conditioning and heating systems are in proper working order before embarking on your journey. Driving in extreme temperatures can be challenging without functional climate control.

- Emergency Kit:

Prepare an emergency kit that includes essential items for potential break-downs or roadside incidents. Your kit should include a flashlight, reflective warning triangles, basic tools like screwdrivers and pliers, a tire pressure gauge, and a first-aid kit. Having these items readily available can help you address minor issues and stay safe until professional assistance arrives.

By attending to these vehicle maintenance tips, you'll be better equipped to enjoy a safe and smooth road trip to Atlanta. The peace of mind that comes with knowing your vehicle is in top-notch condition will allow you to focus on the adventure ahead, savoring the journey and uncovering the hidden gems that await you in this vibrant city. With your vehicle primed and ready, the open road beckons, and your road trip to Atlanta's wonders is about to begin!

2.3 Safety Precautions

Safety should always be a top priority during your road trip to Atlanta. By taking necessary precautions and being vigilant, you can ensure a secure and enjoyable journey. Here are some comprehensive safety tips to keep in mind:

- Seat Belts:

Always wear your seat belt while driving, and ensure that all passengers in your vehicle do the same. Seat belts are your first line of defense in case of an accident and can significantly reduce the risk of injury.

- Speed Limits and Traffic Rules:

Observe and obey posted speed limits and traffic rules at all times. Speeding is a leading cause of accidents, and adhering to traffic regulations will help prevent collisions and ensure a safe driving experience.

- Rest Stops:

Plan regular rest stops during long drives to prevent fatigue and drowsy driving. Fatigue can impair reaction times and decision-making abilities, leading to dangerous situations on the road. Take breaks every two hours or as needed to stretch, hydrate, and refresh.

- Emergency Contacts:

Share your road trip itinerary and contact information with a trusted friend or family member. In the event of an emergency, they will be able to reach you or assist in coordinating help if needed.

- Weather Conditions:

Stay informed about weather conditions along your route, especially during stormy or extreme weather events. Check weather forecasts and advisories before setting out and be prepared to adjust your plans if necessary.

- Fuel Stops:

Plan your fuel stops ahead of time, especially in rural areas with fewer gas stations. It's a good practice to refuel when your tank is about half full, ensuring you don't run out of fuel in remote or rural locations.

- Avoid Distracted Driving:

Distractions while driving can lead to accidents. Avoid using your phone, texting, or engaging in activities that take your focus away from the road. If you need to use your phone for navigation or communication, consider parking or using a hands-free device.

- Follow Local Laws:

Familiarize yourself with local traffic laws and regulations, as they may vary from state to state. Be aware of speed limits, right-of-way rules, and any specific driving laws unique to the areas you'll be traveling through.

- Travel Insurance:

Consider purchasing travel insurance that includes coverage for medical emergencies, trip interruptions, and rental car protection. Travel insurance provides an added layer of security and financial protection in case unforeseen circumstances disrupt your plans.

- Safety in Urban Areas:

When exploring Atlanta's urban areas, be mindful of your surroundings, especially in unfamiliar neighborhoods. Park in well-lit areas and avoid leaving valuables visible inside your vehicle.

- Communication and Navigation:

Ensure that you have a reliable means of communication throughout your road trip. Keep your phone charged and have a car charger on hand. In areas with limited mobile coverage, carry a physical map or GPS device to navigate your route.

- Roadside Assistance:

Join a roadside assistance program or familiarize yourself with the services offered by your insurance provider. Roadside assistance can be invaluable in case of breakdowns, flat tires, or lockouts.

By following these safety precautions, you can enjoy a worry-free and secure road trip to Atlanta. Responsible driving, staying alert, and being prepared for unforeseen situations will enhance your overall road trip experience. Keep in mind that a safe journey is not only about reaching your destination but also about embracing the adventure and creating cherished memories along the way. With safety as your priority, your road trip to Atlanta's hidden gems is sure to be a journey filled with joy, wonder, and unforgettable experiences.

Exploring Atlanta's Hidden Gems

Welcome to Atlanta, a city brimming with hidden gems waiting to be discovered! In this chapter, we'll take you on an exhilarating journey through the lesser-known corners of Atlanta, where culture, history, and creativity intersect to create a tapestry of unique experiences. From charming neighborhoods and cultural hotspots to delectable culinary delights, this comprehensive chapter guide will help you unravel the secrets and treasures that make Atlanta a captivating destination.

3.1 Historic Neighborhoods

Atlanta's historic neighborhoods are a fascinating blend of architectural wonders, cultural landmarks, and community spirit. Each neighborhood tells its own story, reflecting the city's evolution over time. Immerse yourself in the charm of these historic districts as you uncover their unique treasures with the following lists:

- Sweet Auburn:

Once known as the "richest Negro street in the world," Sweet Auburn is a testament to African-American heritage and entrepreneurship. Take a walk down Auburn Avenue, once the epicenter of the civil rights movement and the birthplace of Dr. Martin Luther King Jr. Visit the Martin Luther King Jr. National Historical Park, where you can pay homage to the iconic leader and learn about his life and legacy.

• Cabbagetown:

This artsy neighborhood was once a mill town built to house workers in the nearby cotton mills. Today, it is a haven for artists, musicians, and creatives. Stroll through its narrow streets adorned with colorful murals and charming cottages. Don't miss the Krog Street Tunnel, a vibrant graffiti tunnel that showcases an ever-changing gallery of street art.

• Old Fourth Ward:

As one of Atlanta's oldest neighborhoods, the Old Fourth Ward exudes historic charm and contemporary flair. Discover the historic sites along Edgewood Avenue, including the childhood home of Dr. Martin Luther King Jr. The neighborhood has undergone significant revitalization and is now known for its bustling restaurant scene and popular hangouts along the Eastside BeltLine Trail.

• Castleberry Hill:

A thriving arts district, Castleberry Hill boasts a collection of galleries, studios, and art spaces. Its historic warehouses have been repurposed into creative hubs, making it a vibrant neighborhood for art enthusiasts. Explore the monthly Castleberry Hill Art Stroll to engage with local artists and their diverse works.

- Kirkwood:

Nestled to the east of downtown Atlanta, Kirkwood exudes a small-town feel with tree-lined streets and a close-knit community. Wander through Victorian and Craftsman-style homes, appreciating their architectural beauty. The neighborhood's commercial hub, the Kirkwood Urban Forest, offers green spaces and walking trails for a peaceful escape.

- Reynoldstown:

Reynoldstown's industrial past has given way to a lively neighborhood with a thriving arts scene. Explore the murals and sculptures scattered throughout the area, reflecting its creative spirit. The Atlanta BeltLine Eastside Trail runs through Reynoldstown, making it a popular spot for cyclists and pedestrians.

- West End:

Steeped in history, West End is a historic district with a diverse community and a strong sense of community pride. Visit the West End Historic District, where you can admire the architecture of well-preserved Victorian homes. The neighborhood also hosts the West End BeltLine Market, a bustling farmers' market celebrating local produce and artisans.

Each of these historic neighborhoods in Atlanta offers a distinctive experience that contributes to the city's rich tapestry of culture and heritage. Whether you're an architecture enthusiast, an art lover, or a history buff, exploring these hidden gems will provide you with a deeper appreciation for Atlanta's unique character and the stories of its vibrant communities. So, set out on foot or by bike, and let the hidden corners of Atlanta's past weave their magic as you create unforgettable memories on this enthralling road trip.

3.2 Cultural Hotspots

Atlanta's cultural hotspots showcase the city's dynamic arts scene, historical significance, and commitment to education and human rights. Immerse yourself in these enriching destinations to gain a deeper understanding of Atlanta's cultural diversity and creative expressions:

- Atlanta History Center:

Step into Atlanta's past at the Atlanta History Center, a comprehensive museum complex that offers a glimpse into the city's history, from the Civil War era to the Civil Rights Movement. Explore historic homes, such as the Swan House and Smith Family Farm, and visit the Centennial Olympic Games Museum to relive the 1996 Olympics hosted in Atlanta. The History Center's extensive exhibits and gardens provide an engaging experience for visitors of all ages.

- The Fox Theatre:

As an architectural gem and a historic performing arts venue, The Fox Theatre is a must-visit for theater enthusiasts and architecture aficionados alike. The opulent design, characterized by its Arabian-themed décor, transports visitors to a bygone era of glamour and grandeur. Catch a Broadway show, concert, or ballet performance in this iconic theater that has graced Atlanta's Midtown since 1929.

- Fernbank Museum of Natural History:

Embark on a journey through time at the Fernbank Museum, where exhibits on natural history and science captivate visitors of all ages. Explore the world's largest dinosaur exhibit, take a stroll through the lush Fernbank Forest, and learn about the ecosystems that have shaped Georgia's landscape over millennia.

- Center for Puppetry Arts:

Immerse yourself in the enchanting world of puppetry at the Center for Puppetry Arts. This unique cultural institution celebrates the art of puppetry through engaging performances, workshops, and exhibits. Whether you're a child or a child at heart, you'll be captivated by the artistry and storytelling magic of puppetry.

- Martin Luther King Jr. National Historical Park

This iconic site commemorates the life and legacy of civil rights leader Dr. Martin Luther King Jr. Visit his birth home, Ebenezer Baptist Church, and the King Center, where Dr. King and his wife, Coretta Scott King, are buried. The park serves as a poignant reminder of the fight for equality and justice, inspiring visitors to continue working towards a better future.

- Atlanta Contemporary

As a hub for contemporary art, Atlanta Contemporary showcases thought-provoking works from local, national, and international artists. This non-profit art center features rotating exhibitions, artist talks, and public programs that promote critical conversations about modern artistic expression.

- The Breman Jewish Heritage Museum:

Discover the rich history and cultural contributions of Atlanta's Jewish community at The Breman Museum. Its diverse exhibits explore Jewish heritage, traditions, and stories, fostering a greater understanding of Jewish life in the American South.

3.3 Culinary Delights

Atlanta's culinary scene is a vibrant melting pot of flavors, reflecting the city's diverse cultural influences and culinary innovation. From soulful Southern comfort food to international cuisines, Atlanta offers a delectable array of culinary delights that will leave your taste buds craving for more are:

- Southern Soul Food:

Indulge in the heartwarming flavors of Southern soul food, which has deep roots in Atlanta's culinary heritage. Head to Paschal's Restaurant, a historic soul food institution, to savor classics like fried chicken, collard greens, cornbread, and peach cobbler. Mary Mac's Tea Room is another must-visit for its delightful array of Southern dishes served with a side of Southern hospitality.

- International Cuisine on Buford Highway:

Take a culinary adventure along Buford Highway, Atlanta's renowned "International Corridor." This stretch is a food lover's paradise, boasting a wide variety of authentic ethnic eateries representing cultures from around the world. From Vietnamese pho at Pho Dai Loi to Korean barbecue at Iron Age, and Latin American delights at El Rey del Taco, your taste buds will embark on a global journey.

- Food Halls:

Atlanta's food hall scene is a treasure trove of diverse culinary experiences, all under one roof. Ponce City Market houses a fantastic food hall where you can sample everything from Southern barbecue to artisanal ice cream. Krog Street Market is another foodie haven with a mix of chef-driven stalls and creative concepts, making it the perfect spot to explore new and innovative dishes.

- Innovative Dining Experiences:

For an extraordinary dining experience, explore Atlanta's vibrant restaurant scene, where chefs push the boundaries of culinary creativity. Staplehouse offers a fine-dining experience that blends seasonal ingredients with refined techniques, while Gunshow presents a unique dining concept where chefs circulate the dining room with their creations, giving diners a chance to choose from a rotating selection of inventive dishes.

- Sweet Treats and Desserts:

Indulge your sweet tooth with Atlanta's delightful array of desserts and sweet treats. The Colonnade, a classic Southern eatery, is renowned for its mouthwatering pies, while Sublime Doughnuts offers an irresistible selection of creative doughnut flavors. For artisanal ice cream, visit Jeni's Splendid Ice Creams or Butter & Cream for handcrafted frozen delights.

- Craft Breweries:

Atlanta's craft beer scene is thriving, with numerous breweries offering a wide range of artisanal brews. Pay a visit to SweetWater Brewing Company, one of Atlanta's largest craft breweries, or Monday Night Brewing for a unique tasting experience. Enjoy a refreshing pint in their taprooms while learning about the brewing process.

- Farm-to-Table Delights:

Embrace the farm-to-table movement at restaurants that prioritize fresh, locally sourced ingredients. Local Three Kitchen & Bar and Miller Union are celebrated for their commitment to seasonal, sustainable cuisine that highlights the best of Georgia's produce.

As you embark on this culinary journey, you'll discover that Atlanta's food scene is not just about flavors; it's a reflection of the city's spirit and creativity. From time-honored Southern recipes passed down through generations to 3.4 Outdoor Escapes

- Piedmont Park:

As Atlanta's premier urban park, Piedmont Park is an oasis of greenery and recreation. The park spans over 200 acres and features lush landscapes, walking trails, picnic areas, and sports facilities. Rent a bike or bring a frisbee to engage in friendly games on the open lawns. The picturesque Lake Clara Meer is perfect for leisurely strolls and birdwatching.

- Atlanta BeltLine:

Discover Atlanta's transformation along the Atlanta BeltLine, a revitalized railway corridor converted into a multi-use trail system. The Eastside Trail and Westside Trail offer scenic pathways for walking, jogging, or cycling through diverse neighborhoods and public art installations. Enjoy the vibrant street art and murals that line the BeltLine, adding a colorful touch to your outdoor adventure.

- Chattahoochee River National Recreation Area:

Unwind along the banks of the Chattahoochee River, a serene escape just outside the city. The Chattahoochee River National Recreation Area provides an array of recreational activities, such as kayaking, fishing, and hiking. Explore the numerous trails that wind through wooded areas and along the river's edge, offering breathtaking views of this scenic waterway.

- Arabia Mountain National Heritage Area:

Venture southeast of Atlanta to Arabia Mountain National Heritage Area, a unique landscape of exposed rock outcrops and lush plant life. Take a hike up Arabia Mountain for panoramic views of the surrounding landscape, characterized by its otherworldly beauty. During spring, the area bursts into colorful wildflower displays, creating a stunning backdrop for outdoor enthusiasts and nature photographers.

- Sope Creek Park:

Nestled along the banks of the Chattahoochee River, Sope Creek Park is a hidden gem for hikers and history buffs alike. Explore the park's trails, passing remnants of the old paper mill and the iconic ruins of the Marietta Paper Mill. The picturesque Paper Mill Ruins Trail offers a scenic hike along the river's edge, making it an ideal spot for photography and nature observation.

- Atlanta Botanical Garden:

Immerse yourself in the beauty of nature at the Atlanta Botanical Garden. This urban oasis features a diverse collection of plants and flowers, including themed gardens such as the Japanese Garden and the Rose Garden. Don't miss the Canopy Walk, a treetop adventure that offers a bird's-eye view of the lush gardens below.

- Kennesaw Mountain National Battlefield Park:

History and nature intertwine at Kennesaw Mountain National Battlefield Park, a site where a significant Civil War battle took place. Hike to the summit of Kennesaw Mountain for panoramic views of the area's rolling hills and historic landscapes. The park's extensive trail network provides opportunities to explore the battlefield's historical markers and learn about its significance in American history.

3.5 Festivals and Events

Immerse yourself in the lively spirit of Atlanta by joining in on the city's diverse and vibrant festivals and events. From celebrating arts and culture to reveling in music and entertainment, Atlanta's calendar is packed with exciting gatherings that offer a glimpse into the city's dynamic and inclusive community:

- Atlanta Film Festival:

Film enthusiasts won't want to miss the Atlanta Film Festival, one of the longest-running and most prestigious film festivals in the Southeast. Held annually, this event showcases a diverse selection of independent films from around the world. From thought-provoking documentaries to captivating narratives, the festival screens a wide range of genres that cater to all cinematic tastes.

- Atlanta Jazz Festival:

Experience the soulful sounds of jazz at the Atlanta Jazz Festival, a Memorial Day weekend tradition in the city. This free event attracts music lovers from all walks of life and features performances by acclaimed jazz musicians and local talent. Set against the backdrop of beautiful Piedmont Park, the festival captures the essence of Atlanta's musical heritage.

- Dragon Con:

Calling all science fiction, fantasy, and pop culture enthusiasts! Dragon Con is a multi-genre convention that draws fans, creators, and celebrities from all over the world. Held over Labor Day weekend, this immersive event features panels, workshops, costume parades, and performances celebrating all things geek culture. It's a feast for fans of movies, TV shows, comics, video games, and more.

- Atlanta Dogwood Festival:

Each spring, the Atlanta Dogwood Festival ushers in the season with three days of art, music, and entertainment. Piedmont Park transforms into an outdoor gallery showcasing the works of artists from across the country. The festival also features live music performances, a disc dog competition, and a delightful selection of food vendors.

- Atlanta Food & Wine Festival:

For foodies and wine enthusiasts, the Atlanta Food & Wine Festival is a delectable celebration of Southern cuisine and libations. This culinary extravaganza brings together top chefs, sommeliers, and mixologists for a series of tastings, workshops, and seminars that showcase the region's diverse food culture.

- Music Midtown:

Music lovers rejoice at Music Midtown, a two-day music festival that hosts a lineup of popular and diverse artists from various genres. This annual event, held in Piedmont Park, offers a fantastic opportunity to experience live performances in a lively outdoor setting.

- Atlanta Pride Festival:

Join in on Atlanta's celebration of LGBTQ+ pride and diversity at the Atlanta Pride Festival. This weekend-long event includes a colorful parade, live entertainment, community booths, and parties. It serves as a powerful reminder of Atlanta's commitment to inclusivity and acceptance.

These festivals and events showcase the city's vibrant arts scene, love for music, and celebration of diversity. Embrace the lively atmosphere, make new friends, and immerse yourself in Atlanta's rich cultural tapestry. Attending these gatherings not only allows you to partake in the city's festivities but also provides an opportunity to connect with fellow attendees and experience the warmth and camaraderie that define Atlanta's sense of community. So, mark your calendars and let the energy and excitement of Atlanta's festivals and events ignite your journey of discovery on this road trip like no other.

Captivating Atlanta Museums and Galleries

This Chapter invites you to explore the city's captivating museums and galleries. From art and history to science and innovation, these cultural institutions offer an immersive experience that reveals Atlanta's diverse heritage and creative spirit.

4.1 Atlanta History Center

The Atlanta History Center is a captivating and enriching destination that offers visitors a deep dive into the rich history and culture of Atlanta and the American South. As one of the leading history museums in the region, it showcases an impressive collection of artifacts, exhibits, and interactive displays that span centuries of history, allowing visitors to step back in time and experience the past come to life in the following:

- Historical Exhibits:

The Atlanta History Center boasts a diverse array of historical exhibits that cover various aspects of Atlanta's past. From its founding in the early 19th century to its growth as a major transportation hub during the Civil War and beyond, these exhibits provide a comprehensive overview of the city's evolution.

- Swan House:

One of the centerpieces of the Atlanta History Center is the Swan House, an elegant and stately mansion that dates back to the 1920s. The house's beautifully preserved interiors and lush gardens transport visitors to the golden era of Southern aristocracy.

- Civil War Exhibits:

Given Atlanta's significance during the American Civil War, the history center features extensive exhibits dedicated to this pivotal period. Visitors can explore the war's impact on the city, the stories of soldiers and civilians, and the strategies that shaped the course of the conflict.

- Centennial Olympic Games:

Atlanta played host to the 1996 Summer Olympics, and the history center commemorates this historic event with exhibits showcasing the games' impact on the city and the legacy it left behind.

- Interactive Experiences:

The Atlanta History Center offers interactive experiences that engage visitors of all ages. From hands-on activities for children to immersive multimedia displays, these interactive elements make history come alive and create an engaging learning environment.

- Margaret Mitchell House:

For fans of literature, the history center includes the Margaret Mitchell House, the former home of the Pulitzer Prize-winning author of "Gone with the Wind." The house provides insights into Mitchell's life and work, and visitors can explore the place where this iconic novel was written.

- Tullie Smith Farm:

The Tullie Smith Farm is a living history exhibit, showcasing life in 19th-century Georgia. It features original buildings, including a farmhouse and slave quarters, allowing visitors to experience daily life in a historic Southern farm setting.

- Artifacts and Archives:

The Atlanta History Center houses an extensive collection of artifacts, photographs, documents, and archives that serve as valuable resources for researchers and history enthusiasts alike. These collections offer an in-depth look into the people, events, and moments that shaped Atlanta's history.

- Special Events and Programs:

Throughout the year, the history center hosts a variety of special events, lectures, and programs that delve deeper into specific historical topics. These events provide unique opportunities to engage with experts and gain a deeper understanding of Atlanta's past.

- Gardens and Grounds:

The history center's beautiful gardens and scenic grounds provide a tranquil setting to reflect on the stories and history encountered inside the museum. Strolling through the gardens is a perfect way to unwind after a day of exploration.

4.2 High Museum of Art

The High Museum of Art in Atlanta is a cultural gem and a must-visit destination for art enthusiasts and curious travelers alike. As one of the leading art museums in the Southeastern United States, the High Museum boasts an extensive and diverse collection of artwork spanning various periods and genres, showcasing both American and European art. Founded in 1905, the museum has grown into a renowned institution known for its exceptional exhibitions, educational programs, and captivating architectures making it a cultural hub that continuously inspires and captivates visitors with the following:

- The Collection:

The High Museum's collection encompasses a wide range of art forms, including paintings, sculptures, decorative arts, photography, and more. Visitors can admire works by renowned artists such as Claude Monet, Vincent van Gogh, John Singer Sargent, and Pierre-Auguste Renoir, among many others.

- American Art:

The museum's American art collection showcases the evolution of American art from the late 18th century to the present day. From Hudson River School landscapes to contemporary works, this collection provides a comprehensive overview of American artistic expression.

- European Art:

The European art collection features works from the Renaissance to the 20th century, offering insights into European artistic movements and iconic masterpieces.

- Decorative Arts:

The High Museum's decorative arts collection includes furniture, ceramics, glassware, and textiles, providing a glimpse into the evolution of design and craftsmanship through the ages.

- Photography:

The photography collection is a highlight of the museum, featuring an impressive array of images that capture significant moments in history, showcase artistic innovations, and explore the human experience.

- Special Exhibitions:

In addition to its permanent collection, the High Museum hosts a dynamic lineup of special exhibitions, bringing world-class art and traveling shows to Atlanta. These exhibitions often explore diverse themes, cultures, and artistic movements, making every visit to the museum a unique experience.

- Educational Programs:

The High Museum is committed to providing enriching educational experiences for visitors of all ages. From guided tours and lectures to hands-on workshops and family programs, the museum offers opportunities for learning and engagement with art.

- Richard Meier Building:

The museum's architecture is a work of art in itself. Designed by renowned architect Richard Meier, the building features a striking contemporary design with natural light-filled spaces that provide a perfect setting for the art on display.

- Toddler Thursdays:

For families with young children, Toddler Thursdays is a popular program that offers interactive art experiences and storytelling sessions designed for children aged 2 to 5.

- Community Engagement:

The High Museum actively engages with the local community, collaborating with various organizations to create inclusive and accessible programs that reflect the diversity of Atlanta.

The High Museum of Art is a cultural beacon, enriching the Atlanta community and inspiring visitors from around the world. Whether you're an art aficionado or a curious traveler, a visit to this captivating museum is an opportunity to immerse yourself in the beauty of artistic expression and connect with the universal language of art. With its exceptional collections, diverse exhibitions, and commitment to education, the High Museum continues to be a source of inspiration and wonder for generations to come.

4.3 Center for Civil and Human Rights

The Center for Civil and Human Rights in Atlanta is a powerful and thought-provoking institution dedicated to preserving and showcasing the history and ongoing struggle for civil rights and human rights. Located in the heart of downtown Atlanta, the center serves as an immersive and educational experience that engages visitors in a profound exploration of the past, present, and future of civil rights movements around the world:

• Legacy of the American Civil Rights Movement:

The center's exhibits take visitors on a journey through the American Civil Rights Movement, highlighting key events, influential leaders, and pivotal moments that shaped the fight for racial equality and social justice in the United States.

• Interactive Exhibits:

One of the center's most compelling features is its interactive exhibits, which use multimedia technology and storytelling techniques to offer an emotionally engaging and empathetic experience. These exhibits allow visitors to step into the shoes of civil rights activists and gain a deeper understanding of the challenges they faced.

• The Morehouse College Martin Luther King, Jr. Collection:

The center is home to the Morehouse College Martin Luther King, Jr. Collection, which houses a vast archive of documents and personal items related to the life and work of Dr. Martin Luther King, Jr. This collection provides unique insights into the iconic civil rights leader's legacy and impact.

- Global Human Rights Exhibits:

In addition to focusing on the American Civil Rights Movement, the center also sheds light on human rights struggles around the world. These exhibits connect visitors to the broader global fight for justice, equality, and dignity.

- The Voice to the Voiceless:

The Voice to the Voiceless exhibit is a deeply moving experience that amplifies the stories of individuals who have been marginalized and oppressed. This powerful display gives voice to those who have faced discrimination and highlights the importance of advocating for human rights.

- The Spark of Conviction:

This exhibit examines the power of nonviolent protests and how ordinary individuals can spark social change through collective action and advocacy.

- Engaging Educational Programs:

The center offers educational programs and workshops designed for students and educators, providing opportunities for dialogue, critical thinking, and fostering a deeper understanding of civil and human rights issues.

- Social Justice Gallery:

The Social Justice Gallery features rotating exhibits that address contemporary civil and human rights challenges, inspiring visitors to reflect on their role in creating a more just and equitable society.

- Advocacy and Community Engagement:

The center is actively engaged in advocacy work and community outreach, aiming to be a catalyst for positive change in the local and global community.

- Inspirational Visitors Center:

The center's Visitors Center offers a welcoming space where visitors can reflect on their experience, engage in discussions, and connect with others who share a commitment to civil and human rights.

4.4 Atlanta Contemporary

Atlanta Contemporary is a dynamic and cutting-edge arts institution that plays a pivotal role in the city's vibrant arts scene. As a non-profit contemporary art center, it serves as a platform for emerging and established artists to showcase their innovative works and engage with the community. Located in the historic Westside Arts District, the Atlanta Contemporary offers a thought-provoking and immersive experience for art enthusiasts and curious visitors alike:

- Rotating Contemporary Art Exhibitions:

At the heart of Atlanta Contemporary's mission is its commitment to showcasing contemporary art in all its diverse forms. The center's ever-changing exhibitions feature a wide range of media, from painting and sculpture to photography, video, and performance art. This constant evolution keeps the experience fresh and exciting for returning visitors.

- Focus on Emerging Artists:

Atlanta Contemporary places a strong emphasis on supporting emerging artists, providing them with a platform to share their work and ideas with a broader audience. This commitment to nurturing new talent fosters a dynamic and forward-thinking artistic community.

- Engaging Public Programs:

The center hosts a variety of public programs, including artist talks, panel discussions, performances, and workshops. These events offer opportunities for dialogue and interaction with artists, fostering a deeper understanding of contemporary art practices and ideas.

- Artist Studios:

The center includes onsite artist studios, providing a space for artists to create and experiment with their work. Visitors may have the chance to meet artists in their studios, gaining insights into their creative processes and inspirations.

- Site-Specific Installations:

Atlanta Contemporary occasionally commissions site-specific installations that respond to the unique architecture and atmosphere of the center. These installations create immersive experiences that challenge traditional notions of art and engage visitors on a sensory level.

- Community Engagement:

The center is deeply connected to the local community and actively engages with audiences of all ages through educational programs and outreach initiatives. Workshops, family activities, and school programs foster a sense of curiosity and creativity among diverse audiences.

- Contemporary Art Library:

The center's library houses an impressive collection of art-related books, catalogs, and periodicals, serving as a valuable resource for researchers, students, and art enthusiasts seeking to delve deeper into contemporary art discourse.

- Art Shop:

The Art Shop at Atlanta Contemporary offers a curated selection of artworks, prints, books, and unique gifts created by local and regional artists, providing visitors with the opportunity to support the local art community and take home a piece of contemporary art.

- Collaborative Partnerships:

Atlanta Contemporary collaborates with other cultural institutions, galleries, and organizations, creating a network that strengthens the city's arts ecosystem and fosters cross-disciplinary exchanges.

• Artistic Residencies:

The center occasionally hosts artistic residencies, inviting artists from different backgrounds and disciplines to work on projects and engage with the local community. These residencies contribute to a vibrant and inclusive arts dialogue in Atlanta.

4.5 Michael C. Carlos Museum

The Michael C. Carlos Museum, situated on the campus of Emory University in Atlanta, is a treasure trove of art and artifacts from ancient civilizations around the world. Founded in 1919, the museum has grown into one of the premier institutions of its kind in the Southeastern United States. Named in honor of philanthropist Michael C. Carlos, the museum's vast collection spans millennia, offering visitors a captivating journey through the art, history, and culture of ancient civilizations,the must see includes:

• Ancient Art and Artifacts:

The museum's collection features a diverse array of ancient art and artifacts from various cultures, including ancient Egypt, Greece, Rome, the Near East, and the Americas. Visitors can explore sculptures, pottery, jewelry, textiles, and other objects that provide insights into the daily lives, beliefs, and artistic achievements of these civilizations.

• Egyptian Art:

The Carlos Museum houses one of the most extensive collections of ancient Egyptian art in the Southeast. From mummies and funerary masks to monumental statues and delicate amulets, the Egyptian galleries offer a glimpse into the fascinating world of the pharaohs and the afterlife.

- Classical Antiquities:

The museum's classical antiquities collection includes Greek and Roman art, showcasing masterpieces that highlight the artistic achievements and mythological narratives of these ancient civilizations.

- Ancient Near East:

The Near Eastern collection features artifacts from Mesopotamia, Persia, and other ancient cultures, shedding light on the achievements of these early societies and their enduring impact on human history.

- Art of the Americas:

The museum's Art of the Americas collection presents the artistic heritage of pre-Columbian cultures, including the Maya, Aztec, and Inca civilizations. The artifacts on display reveal the sophistication and artistic prowess of these ancient societies.

- Temporary Exhibitions:

In addition to its permanent collections, the Carlos Museum hosts rotating exhibitions that feature art and artifacts from different periods and cultures. These exhibitions offer fresh perspectives and new insights into ancient civilizations and contemporary art practices.

- Educational Programs:

The museum offers a variety of educational programs for visitors of all ages, including lectures, workshops, guided tours, and school programs. These programs provide enriching experiences that foster a deeper understanding and appreciation of ancient art and culture.

- Conservation and Research:

The Carlos Museum is committed to the preservation and study of its collections. The museum's conservation and research efforts contribute to a broader understanding of ancient civilizations and their legacy.

- Carlos Reads:

Carlos Reads is a book club hosted by the museum, focusing on literature related to the ancient world. This engaging program allows participants to explore ancient cultures through literary works and discussions.

- Museum Shop:

The museum's gift shop offers a selection of unique and art-inspired items, including books, jewelry, and gifts that allow visitors to take home a piece of ancient history.

4.6 Fernbank Museum of Natural History

The Fernbank Museum of Natural History in Atlanta is a captivating destination that celebrates the wonders of the natural world and the history of our planet. Located in a lush forested setting, the museum offers a unique blend of immersive exhibits, awe-inspiring artifacts, and engaging educational programs that appeal to visitors of all ages. With a focus on science, discovery, and environmental stewardship, Fernbank Museum provides an enriching and entertaining experience for curious minds and nature enthusiasts alike:

• Giants of the Mesozoic:

One of the museum's most iconic exhibits is "Giants of the Mesozoic," which features a stunning display of life-sized dinosaur models in an immersive Cretaceous-era environment. This exhibit transports visitors back in time to an age when dinosaurs roamed the Earth, offering an unforgettable encounter with these prehistoric giants.

• A Walk Through Time in Georgia:

This exhibit traces the geological history of Georgia, showcasing the region's diverse landscapes and the changes that have shaped the state over millions of years. From ancient marine environments to Ice Age habitats, visitors can explore the rich natural heritage of the region.

• Sensing Nature:

Fernbank Museum encourages interactive learning through its "Sensing

Nature" exhibit, which engages visitors in activities that appeal to their senses. Through touchable specimens, scent stations, and interactive displays, this exhibit provides a hands-on experience that fosters a deeper connection with the natural world.

- Reflections of Culture:

This exhibit explores the cultural diversity of different regions and communities worldwide, highlighting their relationships with nature and the ways they interact with their environments. It offers a broader perspective on human history and the interconnectedness of cultures and ecosystems.

- WildWoods and Fernbank Forest:

The museum's outdoor spaces, including the WildWoods and Fernbank Forest, provide opportunities for exploration and connection with nature. Fernbank Forest is a rare urban old-growth forest that offers hiking trails, wildlife observation, and a chance to experience the beauty of the natural environment.

- Special Exhibitions:

Fernbank Museum hosts a rotating roster of special exhibitions that cover a wide range of natural history topics, from biodiversity and conservation to paleontology and space exploration. These exhibits offer fresh perspectives and keep the museum experience dynamic and engaging.

- IMAX Theatre:

The museum's IMAX Theatre presents captivating nature documentaries and educational films on a massive screen, providing an immersive cinematic experience that complements the museum's mission of inspiring curiosity about the natural world.

- Educational Programs:

Fernbank Museum offers educational programs for families, school groups, and educators, providing enriching experiences that foster a love for science, discovery, and environmental stewardship.

- Family Fun Days and Events:

Throughout the year, the museum hosts family-friendly events, such as themed Family Fun Days and Night at the Museum events, which provide interactive and entertaining experiences for visitors of all ages.

- Fernbank After Dark:

For adult visitors, Fernbank After Dark is a monthly event that offers an opportunity to explore the museum after hours, with activities, music, and cocktails, creating a unique and social experience.

Exploring Atlanta's Highlights

5.1 Downtown Delights

Welcome to downtown Atlanta, the beating heart of the city's bustling urban core. As you explore this vibrant district, you'll find a perfect blend of history, entertainment, and green spaces that cater to a diverse range of interests.

Centennial Olympic Park, created as part of the 1996 Summer Olympics legacy, remains a symbol of Atlanta's transformation and renewal. The park's iconic Fountain of Rings is a popular spot for visitors, especially during the warm months when interactive water shows captivate the audience with choreographed displays.

Adjacent to Centennial Olympic Park stands the Mercedes-Benz Stadium, a modern architectural wonder and home to the Atlanta Falcons NFL team and Atlanta United FC MLS team. Even if you're not attending a game or concert, consider taking a guided tour of the stadium to witness its state-of-the-art features and learn about its sustainable design.

For an unparalleled aquatic experience, head to the Georgia Aquarium, a world-class attraction known for its diverse marine life and innovative exhibits. From beluga whales to colorful tropical fish, the aquarium offers a mesmerizing journey through the wonders of the deep seas.

To get a taste of Atlanta's cultural diversity, venture into Sweet Auburn, a historic African American neighborhood known for its vibrant street life and significant contributions to the city's civil rights movement. You'll find a mix of shops, restaurants, and cultural landmarks, including the historic Big Bethel AME Church and the Auburn Avenue Research Library on African American Culture and History.

In the evening, explore the Downtown dining scene, which boasts a range of restaurants and eateries offering flavors from around the world. From upscale fine dining to food trucks serving delectable street food, there's something to satisfy every palate.

As you navigate the streets of downtown Atlanta, keep an eye out for various events and festivals that often take place here. From music festivals to food fairs and cultural celebrations, there's always something exciting happening in this vibrant and dynamic area.

With its mix of history, entertainment, and cultural attractions, downtown Atlanta stands as a testament to the city's growth and transformation over the years. Embrace the energy, diversity, and captivating spirit of this downtown hub as you embark on your unforgettable journey through Atlanta's highlights.

5.2 Historic Landmarks

Atlanta's rich history is beautifully preserved through its historic landmarks, each offering a glimpse into the city's past and the events that shaped it.

The Atlanta History Center, a sprawling complex located in Buckhead, serves as a treasure trove of Atlanta's heritage. Explore its fascinating exhibits that detail the city's founding, Civil War-era history, and development into a modern metropolis. The center also houses the Swan House, an elegant mansion showcasing the lifestyle of Atlanta's elite during the early 20th century.

For a more somber yet essential visit, make your way to the Oakland Cemetery. Established in 1850, this tranquil resting place is the final resting spot for many prominent figures in Atlanta's history, including Margaret Mitchell, author of the iconic novel "Gone with the Wind." Stroll through its serene gardens, elaborate mausoleums, and beautifully crafted headstones, and gain insights into the lives of the city's past residents.

The Fox Theatre, located on Peachtree Street, stands as a magnificent testament to Atlanta's cultural heritage. This historic movie palace, opened in 1929, showcases a stunning blend of Islamic, Egyptian, and Moorish architectural styles. The Fox Theatre continues to host a wide array of events, from Broadway shows and concerts to film screenings, drawing in visitors from all walks of life.

A short drive away from downtown, you'll find the Martin Luther King Jr. National Historical Park. This revered site pays tribute to the iconic civil rights leader, Dr. Martin Luther King Jr. Explore the visitor center, which houses powerful exhibits, photographs, and artifacts chronicling Dr. King's life and the civil rights movement. Take a walk along the "I Have a Dream" World Peace Rose Garden and visit the Historic Ebenezer Baptist Church, where Dr. King served as co-pastor.

Another architectural marvel worth visiting is the Margaret Mitchell House, the former residence of the Pulitzer Prize-winning author. This Tudor Revival-style house in Midtown Atlanta offers guided tours that provide insight into the life and works of Margaret Mitchell and her creation of the beloved novel "Gone with the Wind."

Atlanta's historic landmarks offer a captivating journey through time, providing an opportunity to reflect on the city's past while celebrating its diverse cultural heritage. Whether you're a history enthusiast or simply curious about the city's roots, these landmarks will leave a lasting impression and deepen your appreciation for Atlanta's unique story.

5.3 Vibrant Neighborhoods

Atlanta is a city of distinct and diverse neighborhoods, each with its unique character and charm. From historic districts to trendy urban hotspots, exploring the city's vibrant neighborhoods offers a rich tapestry of experiences with the following:

- Little Five Points:

Little Five Points, often referred to as L5P, is a bohemian and eclectic neighborhood located east of downtown. This artsy enclave is known for its vibrant street art, vintage shops, record stores, and funky boutiques. Explore the diverse dining options, grab a cup of coffee, and soak in the creative atmosphere. The variety of live music venues and alternative entertainment make Little Five Points a go-to spot for artistic expression and cultural diversity.

- Buford Highway:

For a taste of international flavors, head to Buford Highway. This vibrant stretch is a melting pot of diverse cultures, offering an array of authentic restaurants, markets, and shops representing different cuisines from around the world. From Vietnamese pho to Korean barbecue, Mexican taquerias to Indian curry houses, Buford Highway is a food lover's paradise and a celebration of Atlanta's multicultural culinary scene.

- Virginia-Highland:

Virginia-Highland, or simply VaHi, is a trendy and walkable neighborhood filled with tree-lined streets, charming bungalows, and a bustling commercial district. Boutique shops, upscale dining, and lively bars are scattered throughout the area. Take a leisurely stroll through the neighborhood and enjoy the friendly atmosphere, especially during the annual Virginia-Highland Summerfest, a popular arts and music festival that brings the community together.

- Inman Park:

One of Atlanta's oldest neighborhoods, Inman Park, is a perfect blend of historic charm and modern living. Stroll along the streets lined with beautifully restored Victorian-era homes and lush parks. The neighborhood's highlight is the Inman Park Festival, a yearly event that attracts locals and visitors alike with its artist market, live music, and street parade.

- West Midtown:

West Midtown, also known as Westside or the Westside Design District, has transformed into a thriving hub for creativity and innovation. Former industrial spaces have been repurposed into trendy art galleries, breweries, and chic eateries. Experience the cutting-edge art scene, and enjoy a culinary adventure at the restaurants that exemplify Atlanta's reputation as a food-forward city.

- East Atlanta Village (EAV):

East Atlanta Village is an eclectic and laid-back neighborhood with a strong sense of community. Known for its quirky street art and welcoming vibe, EAV offers a mix of bars, music venues, and boutique shops. Enjoy live performances, open-mic nights, and the neighborhood's friendly charm that makes it a beloved spot for locals and visitors alike.

Hidden Gems Off the Beaten Path

This chapter offers a delightful journey into the lesser-known corners of Atlanta. By exploring nature escapes, quirky attractions, and local eateries, in this chapter you'll uncover the city's hidden treasures and unique charm.

6.1 Nature Escapes

Atlanta's hidden nature escapes offer a myriad of opportunities to connect with the natural beauty of the region. One such gem is the Arabia Mountain National Heritage Area. This unique landscape features exposed granite outcrops, creating a surreal environment reminiscent of a moonscape. Hike along the Arabia Mountain National Heritage Area Trail, and witness breathtaking views of rare plant species and fascinating rock formations.

For a peaceful retreat within the city, visit the Atlanta BeltLine Eastside Trail. This multi-use trail winds through several neighborhoods and parks, providing a scenic pathway for walking, jogging, or biking. Along the trail, you'll encounter public art installations, community gardens, and lovely urban green spaces.

Another hidden natural gem is Cascade Springs Nature Preserve, located southwest of the city. This serene oasis boasts cascading waterfalls, lush forests, and meandering trails, providing an ideal escape from the urban buzz.

It's an excellent spot for a tranquil picnic or a leisurely hike surrounded by nature's tranquility.

For a unique ecological experience, head to the Fernbank Forest, an old-growth forest in the heart of Atlanta. Managed by the Fernbank Museum of Natural History, this urban forest showcases a diverse range of native plant and animal species. Explore the interpretive trails and discover the beauty and biodiversity that thrives amidst the cityscape.

If you're seeking a more adventurous outing, venture to the Vickery Creek Trail at the Chattahoochee River National Recreation Area. This hidden gem is tucked away in the northern suburbs of Atlanta and offers opportunities for hiking, kayaking, and exploring historic ruins along the river.

From the otherworldly landscapes of Arabia Mountain to the peaceful retreats of the Atlanta BeltLine and Cascade Springs, Atlanta's hidden nature escapes promise a rejuvenating experience for outdoor enthusiasts and nature lovers alike. These lesser-known gems offer a chance to step away from the city's hustle and immerse yourself in the serenity of Georgia's natural wonders.

6.2 Quirky and Unique Attractions

Atlanta's charm lies not only in its famous landmarks but also in its lesser-known quirky attractions that add a touch of whimsy and surprise to your exploration.

Head to the Krog Street Tunnel, an underpass covered in vibrant and ever-changing street art. Artists continuously add new graffiti and murals, making it a dynamic and creative canvas reflecting Atlanta's urban culture.

For a step back in time and a dash of nostalgia, visit the Clermont Lounge. This historic nightclub is one of the oldest in Atlanta and is famous for its diverse cast of dancers, including the iconic Blondie, a beloved performer known for her entertaining style and humor.

Make your way to the Center for Love and Light, a spiritual and healing center that offers a unique experience for those seeking alternative therapies and workshops. From yoga classes to sound baths and holistic healing sessions, this hidden gem provides a sanctuary for self-discovery and growth.

Art enthusiasts will appreciate the Bicycle Wheel Tree, a quirky sculpture located in the Cabbagetown neighborhood. This whimsical installation is made up of old bicycle wheels that create a visually striking and playful piece of public art.

Lastly, don't miss the chance to visit the Doll's Head Trail at Constitution Lakes Park. This trail showcases an art installation featuring sculptures made from discarded toys and found objects, all created by local artists. It's an unusual and thought-provoking experience that transforms discarded materials into works of art, reflecting Atlanta's commitment to creativity and sustainability.

From the ever-changing art of the Krog Street Tunnel to the eclectic charm of the Clermont Lounge and the artistic reuse of materials at Doll's Head Trail, Atlanta's quirky and unique attractions will surprise and delight visitors seeking an offbeat and memorable experience. These hidden gems add an extra layer of character to the city, showcasing its vibrant and diverse cultural landscape.

6.3 Local Eateries and Foodie Adventures

Atlanta's culinary scene is a melting pot of flavors and diverse cuisines, making it a haven for food enthusiasts. Delve into the city's local eateries and embark on a gastronomic adventure you won't soon forget.

Head to the Buford Highway Farmers Market, a food lover's paradise with an extensive selection of international foods and ingredients. Explore the sprawling aisles filled with fresh produce, exotic spices, and specialty items from around the world. Savor unique flavors and discover new ingredients to incorporate into your home cooking.

For a taste of classic Southern dishes elevated to a gourmet level, make your way to Staplehouse. This award-winning restaurant not only serves delectable dishes but also supports a charitable cause. Their "Doing Good" program donates profits to The Giving Kitchen, a non-profit organization that assists restaurant workers facing crises.

To experience the vibrant food truck culture in Atlanta, head to the Atlanta Food Truck Park & Market. This bustling venue hosts a rotating selection of food trucks, offering a diverse array of cuisines and inventive dishes. From gourmet sliders to artisanal ice cream sandwiches, the food truck park is a fantastic spot to sample the city's culinary creativity on wheels.

For a taste of Atlanta's contemporary Southern cuisine, book a table at Gunshow. This innovative restaurant, led by acclaimed chef Kevin Gillespie, offers a unique dining experience where chefs bring their creations directly to your table, allowing you to choose your favorites from a constantly evolving menu.

For dessert lovers, visit The Varsity, a beloved Atlanta institution since 1928. This iconic drive-in diner is famous for its hot dogs, burgers, and "Frosted Orange" milkshakes. Experience the nostalgia of a bygone era and enjoy a classic meal at one of the world's largest drive-ins.

Venture into Atlanta's East Asian community by visiting the Buford Highway area, where you'll find an abundance of authentic Vietnamese, Korean,

Chinese, and Thai restaurants. Savor delicious pho, indulge in Korean barbecue, and explore the diverse flavors of Asian street food.

Atlanta's local eateries offer not only a culinary journey but also an immersion into the city's vibrant food culture and community. Whether you're a foodie seeking unique ingredients, innovative dishes, or classic Southern comfort food, Atlanta's diverse culinary landscape promises an unforgettable foodie adventure.

Immersing in Local Culture

Atlanta, is the cultural hub of the American South, invites travelers to immerse themselves in its rich heritage and vibrant local culture. Beyond its famous landmarks and attractions, this bustling metropolis offers a tapestry of experiences that showcase its diverse arts, music, festivals, and unique traditions. This chapter explores the essence of Atlanta's local culture, presenting a colorful array of events, festivals, art scenes, and shopping districts that provide an authentic and unforgettable encounter with the city's soul. From joining in the festivities of annual celebrations to exploring the dynamic art and music scenes, and discovering one-of-a-kind souvenirs, this chapter unveils the true heart of Atlanta and celebrates its distinctive identity as a city that embraces its past while embracing the future.

7.1 Events and Festivals

Atlanta comes alive throughout the year with a diverse array of events and festivals that celebrate its cultural richness and sense of community. These lively gatherings offer a chance to connect with locals, experience traditions, and share in the city's vibrant spirit.

One of the city's most anticipated events is the Atlanta Dogwood Festival, held annually in Piedmont Park during the blooming of the dogwood trees. This lively festival features an impressive art market showcasing the works of talented artists, live music performances, delicious food vendors, and family-friendly activities. The event creates a wonderful opportunity to appreciate Atlanta's artistic side and enjoy the outdoors amidst the beauty of springtime.

In the summer, don't miss the Atlanta Jazz Festival, one of the country's oldest free jazz festivals. Held in Piedmont Park and other venues around the city, this celebration brings together local and international jazz musicians, captivating audiences with soulful performances and the spirit of improvisation.

To experience the cultural diversity of Atlanta, join in the festivities of the Atlanta International Night Market. This annual event showcases the city's global culinary scene, featuring an assortment of food vendors representing various cultures, live music, dance performances, and artisanal goods from around the world. It's a culinary journey that transcends borders and celebrates Atlanta's status as an international melting pot.

For a celebration of LGBTQ+ pride and unity, be a part of the Atlanta Pride Festival, one of the largest pride events in the Southeast. This vibrant and colorful festival includes a colorful parade, live entertainment, educational programs, and a marketplace showcasing LGBTQ+-owned businesses and organizations. It's a time to embrace inclusivity and support the city's LGBTQ+ community.

As autumn approaches, indulge in the lively atmosphere of the Little Five Points Halloween Festival and Parade. This eccentric event draws locals and visitors dressed in creative costumes for a day of spooky fun. Enjoy live music, street performances, and a lively parade that showcases the neighborhood's bohemian and artistic vibe.

7.2 Art and Music Scene

Atlanta's art and music scene pulsate with creativity and diversity, reflecting the city's dynamic cultural landscape. From world-class museums and galleries to iconic music venues, the city offers a rich tapestry of artistic experiences that cater to every taste.

Begin your artistic journey at the High Museum of Art, the Southeast's leading art museum. With an impressive collection spanning from classic to contemporary art, the High Museum showcases works by renowned artists from around the world. Its unique architectural design, crafted by Pritzker Prize-winning architect Richard Meier, adds to the allure of artistic exploration.

For a taste of cutting-edge contemporary art, head to the Atlanta Contemporary Art Center. This non-profit gallery is a haven for avant-garde and experimental art, showcasing the works of emerging and established artists. The center's rotating exhibitions and thought-provoking installations challenge conventional boundaries and inspire dialogue on contemporary issues.

Music enthusiasts will find their rhythm in Atlanta's lively music scene. Historic venues like The Fox Theatre, a 1920s movie palace, offer an enchanting ambiance for concerts and performances, making it a must-visit destination for music lovers of all genres.

To experience Atlanta's soulful roots, venture into local clubs and bars in neighborhoods like Little Five Points and East Atlanta Village. Here, you'll discover an array of live music venues hosting talented local musicians and bands, creating an authentic and intimate setting for live performances.

Immerse yourself in the city's rich musical legacy by visiting the birthplace of

Martin Luther King Jr., the Sweet Auburn neighborhood. This vibrant area, with its roots deeply tied to the civil rights movement, played a pivotal role in the history of American music, nurturing the development of gospel, blues, and soul music.

For an extraordinary musical experience, attend the Atlanta Symphony Orchestra's performances. This world-class orchestra, based at the Woodruff Arts Center, showcases exceptional talent and offers a diverse repertoire ranging from classical masterpieces to contemporary works.

Atlanta's art and music scene beckon travelers to explore the city's creative spirit and immerse themselves in its cultural expressions. From contemporary art to soul-stirring melodies, the art and music scene in Atlanta is a testament to the city's vibrant and ever-evolving cultural identity. Whether you're a seasoned art enthusiast or a music aficionado, Atlanta's artistic offerings promise to leave an indelible mark on your road trip experience.

7.3 Souvenirs and Shopping

Atlanta offers a treasure trove of souvenirs and shopping experiences that allow you to take a piece of the city's vibrant culture and creativity home with you.

For unique and handcrafted mementos, visit the Indie Craft Experience. This local market showcases the works of talented artisans, featuring an array of handmade crafts, jewelry, home décor, and accessories. Supporting local artists and makers, this market allows you to find one-of-a-kind pieces that embody the spirit of Atlanta.

For a taste of Southern flavors and artisanal goods, head to the Sweet Auburn Curb Market. This historic market is a foodie's paradise, offering an assortment of local produce, gourmet treats, and specialty foods. From locally roasted coffee to homemade jams and baked goods, the market is an excellent spot to savor the diverse flavors of Atlanta.

For a curated selection of gifts and home décor, explore the shops in the trendy Virginia-Highland neighborhood. Here, you'll find boutique stores offering a mix of unique gifts, clothing, and accessories that reflect the neighborhood's eclectic and bohemian vibe.

To experience the local food scene through your shopping, visit the Buford Highway Farmers Market. In addition to fresh produce, this market offers an extensive selection of international ingredients, spices, and unique food items that will inspire your culinary adventures long after you leave the city.

For book lovers, a visit to the A Cappella Books is a must. This independent bookstore, located in the Little Five Points neighborhood, offers a diverse collection of new and used books across various genres. Pick up a book by a local author or discover a hidden gem that resonates with your interests.

Atlanta's shopping experiences allow you to support local businesses and artisans while exploring the city's creativity and cultural diversity. Whether you're seeking souvenirs that capture Atlanta's spirit, unique gifts for loved ones, or simply browsing for delightful finds, the city's shopping scene promises a rewarding and memorable experience.

Accommodations and Rest Stops

As you embark on your road trip adventure through diverse highlights and gems, finding the perfect accommodations and rest stops along the way is essential to ensure a comfortable and rejuvenating journey.This Chapter is your guide to discovering a range of lodging options, from luxurious hotels and cozy bed and breakfasts to picturesque campgrounds and RV parks. Whether you prefer immersing in the heart of the city or seeking serenity in nature, this chapter offers a selection of accommodations that cater to every traveler's preferences.

8.1 Hotels, Inns, and Resorts

Atlanta offers a wide range of accommodations, from luxurious hotels to charming inns and resorts, ensuring that every traveler finds a comfortable and convenient place to stay.

For a luxurious and elegant experience, consider staying at one of the city's renowned hotels, such as The Ritz-Carlton or the Four Seasons Atlanta. These five-star establishments offer impeccable service, opulent amenities, and a central location, making them ideal choices for travelers seeking a lavish and sophisticated stay in the heart of the city.

For a more intimate and boutique atmosphere, explore the charming inns and boutique hotels scattered throughout Atlanta's neighborhoods. In areas like Midtown, Buckhead, and Virginia-Highland, you'll find charming bed and breakfasts that exude warmth and hospitality. These smaller accommodations provide personalized service, cozy rooms, and a home-away-from-home ambiance.

If you prefer to escape the city's hustle and immerse yourself in nature, consider one of Atlanta's picturesque resorts. Located just outside the city, resorts like the Chateau Elan Winery & Resort or the Barnsley Resort offer a tranquil retreat amidst beautiful landscapes. Enjoy amenities such as spa facilities, golf courses, and outdoor activities while experiencing the peaceful allure of the countryside.

For travelers seeking a more budget-friendly option, Atlanta also offers a variety of well-known hotel chains that provide comfortable and affordable accommodations. Many of these hotels are conveniently located near major highways, making them convenient rest stops during your road trip.

No matter your preferences or budget, Atlanta's diverse array of hotels, inns, and resorts ensures that you'll find the perfect place to relax and recharge during your road trip adventure. Whether you choose to indulge in luxury or embrace the charm of a cozy inn, your accommodation in Atlanta will complement your exploration of the city's highlights and hidden gems, making your journey even more memorable and enjoyable.

8.2 Camping and RV Parks

For travelers who crave a more adventurous and nature-centric experience, Atlanta offers a range of camping and RV parks that allow you to immerse yourself in the great outdoors.

Sweetwater Creek State Park, located just west of Atlanta, is a popular destination for camping enthusiasts. The park's serene surroundings, hiking trails, and picturesque lake provide an idyllic setting for camping under the stars. Enjoy the peaceful ambiance and the soothing sound of the creek as you unwind in nature.

If you prefer a camping experience near the city, consider Stone Mountain Park. This massive park, home to the iconic Stone Mountain, offers numerous camping options, including tent and RV sites. Wake up to stunning views of the mountain and enjoy the park's attractions, including hiking trails, a scenic railroad, and a laser light show.

Jones RV Park is another excellent choice for RV travelers. Situated in Norcross, just north of Atlanta, this park offers full hookup sites and convenient amenities such as laundry facilities and Wi-Fi. It provides a relaxing spot to rest and recharge during your road trip.

For those seeking a more rustic camping experience, venture to Chattahoochee Bend State Park. Located southwest of Atlanta, this park offers tent camping sites along the Chattahoochee River, allowing you to enjoy the beauty of the riverfront and explore the park's nature trails.

If you're traveling in an RV and prefer a full-service campground, consider Atlanta South RV Resort. This resort-style campground provides spacious sites, modern amenities, and a friendly atmosphere, making it a comfortable base for your Atlanta adventures.

Camping and RV parks in and around Atlanta offer a chance to escape the urban bustle and experience the beauty of Georgia's natural landscapes. Whether you're camping in a tent or traveling in an RV, these parks provide a sense of tranquility and a deeper connection to the region's natural wonders. Embrace the spirit of adventure and sleep under the stars as you create unforgettable memories during your Atlanta road trip.

8.3 Cozy Bed and Breakfasts

For travelers seeking a warm and welcoming stay with a personal touch, Atlanta's cozy bed and breakfasts offer a charming and intimate experience.

Inman Park Bed and Breakfast is a delightful choice for those who appreciate historic charm and a central location. Located in the Inman Park neighborhood, this beautifully restored Victorian-era house provides elegant rooms, delicious homemade breakfast, and easy access to local shops and restaurants.

For a romantic retreat, consider the Shellmont Inn Bed and Breakfast in Midtown. This historic mansion exudes Southern hospitality and offers well-appointed rooms, lush gardens, and a relaxing atmosphere. Indulge in a gourmet breakfast served in the formal dining room or on the veranda, creating a memorable start to your day.

In the Virginia-Highland neighborhood, the Sugar Magnolia Bed & Breakfast welcomes guests with its inviting and comfortable ambiance. The inn's cozy rooms, adorned with antiques and unique décor, provide a charming home away from home. Enjoy a delicious breakfast in the sunny dining room or on the outdoor patio, surrounded by beautiful gardens.

For a peaceful retreat outside the city, the Claremont House Bed and Breakfast in Rome, Georgia, is a hidden gem. Set amidst rolling hills and historic architecture, this antebellum-style inn offers a serene escape from the hustle of city life. Enjoy afternoon tea on the veranda and immerse yourself in the beauty of the surrounding countryside.

The Stonehurst Place Bed and Breakfast, located in the heart of Midtown, provides an eco-friendly and luxurious experience. This beautifully restored mansion boasts contemporary artwork and modern amenities, offering a unique fusion of history and comfort. Savor gourmet breakfasts and afternoon wine and cheese tastings during your stay.

Cozy bed and breakfasts in Atlanta offer more than just comfortable accommodations; they provide a personal and authentic touch that elevates your road trip experience. With friendly innkeepers, unique and charming surroundings, and delicious homemade breakfasts, these bed and breakfasts create an ambiance of warmth and relaxation, ensuring that you'll feel right at home during your Atlanta adventure.

Making Memories Road Trip Stories

E very road trip is filled with moments of wonder, spontaneity, and discovery.This Chapter invites you to share in the enchanting tales of fellow road-trippers and their unforgettable experiences in Atlanta. From chance encounters with friendly locals to breathtaking encounters with nature's wonders, these road trip stories paint a vivid tapestry of adventures and cherished memories. Delve into the heartwarming and exhilarating accounts of personal triumphs, hidden gems unearthed, and the joy of embarking on a journey of a lifetime.This Chapter captures the essence of the road trip spirit, reminding us that the true magic of travel lies not only in the destinations we reach but also in the serendipitous and transformative moments that unfold along the way.

9.1 Reader Contributions

We celebrate the vibrant community of road-trippers who have ventured through Atlanta and experienced its many wonders firsthand. This is dedicated to the heartfelt and captivating contributions from readers like you, who graciously share their road trip stories, making this chapter a treasure trove of personal narratives and cherished memories.

From thrilling encounters on the road to heartwarming moments of con-nection with locals, each reader's contribution is a unique reflection of their journey through Atlanta's diverse landscapes and hidden gems. These tales capture the essence of adventure and the thrill of exploration, serving as a source of inspiration and camaraderie for fellow travelers.

Reader contributions exemplify the magic of road trips - the magic of weaving together our individual experiences into a shared tapestry of adventure and exploration. As you immerse yourself in these tales, you'll be transported to the open roads of Atlanta, feeling the excitement and the sense of wonder that accompanies every road trip.

9.2 Personal Road Trip Experiences

Each personal road trip experience is a unique narrative, a glimpse into the heart and soul of the traveler, and a testament to the transformative power of travel. From solo adventurers seeking self-discovery to families bonding over shared experiences, these stories embody the essence of the road trip spirit - the joy of venturing into the unknown, the thrill of spontaneity, and the profound connections forged along the way.

As you immerse yourself in these personal accounts, you'll witness the beauty of chance encounters with fellow travelers, the awe of discovering hidden natural gems, and the enchantment of stumbling upon charming local events and festivals. Each narrative serves as a testament to the unpredictability and magic that infuses every road trip, reminding us that the journey itself is as valuable as the destination.

These personal road trip experiences offer a glimpse into the soulful connections forged with places, people, and the self. They remind us that the road trip is not just about crossing miles on a map but about embarking on a transformative adventure that leaves an indelible mark on our hearts.

Join us as we celebrate the rich tapestry of personal road trip experiences, each woven with the threads of curiosity, courage, and wonder. May these stories inspire you to embark on your own road trip adventure through Atlanta, knowing that within every journey lies the potential for profound connections and unforgettable memories.

Practical Tips and Resources

As you embark on your road trip adventure through Atlanta's enchanting landscapes and cultural treasures, This Chapter is your compass to practical tips and invaluable resources that will enhance your journey. From budgeting wisely to staying connected on the go and leveraging helpful apps and websites, this chapter equips you with essential tools to navigate your road trip with ease and confidence.

10.1 Budgeting Your Road Trip

Budgeting for a road trip requires careful planning and consideration of various expenses. From fuel costs to accommodations, food, and activities, each aspect demands thoughtful allocation of resources. We will provide practical tips to help you plan your road trip budget effectively, allowing you to strike a balance between exploration and financial responsibility:

- Researching and comparing fuel prices along your route can save you significant funds during your journey. Mapping out your itinerary and calculating approximate fuel costs will empower you to allocate your budget wisely, ensuring that you have enough resources to explore the places that captivate your heart.

- Consider alternative lodging options, such as camping or staying at budget-friendly motels, to stretch your accommodation budget further. Embrace the charm of Atlanta's cozy bed and breakfasts or explore camping and RV parks, which provide unique experiences while being gentle on your wallet.

- Sampling local cuisine at affordable eateries and food trucks allows you to savor the city's culinary delights without breaking the bank. Exploring farmers' markets and preparing your meals on the go can also be a cost-effective and enjoyable way to embrace Atlanta's food scene.

- To make the most of your activities and attractions, look for discounts, coupons, and free events. Many attractions offer special deals on certain days or during specific times, allowing you to immerse yourself in Atlanta's cultural gems without straining your budget.

- Remember to set aside a contingency fund for unexpected expenses, such as car repairs or unforeseen detours. This cushion ensures that you can handle any surprises that may arise during your road trip.

By prioritizing and optimizing your expenses, you can savor the magic of Atlanta's road trip experience without unnecessary financial stress. Embrace the joy of discovering hidden gems, immersing in local culture, and making lifelong memories, all while staying within your budget. Chapter 9.1 equips you with the tools to craft a budget that empowers you to explore with financial freedom, ensuring that your Atlanta road trip is not only unforgettable but also financially sound.

10.2 Staying Connected on the Go

Staying connected on the go is crucial for safety, convenience, and sharing your journey with family and friends. Consider investing in a reliable mobile hotspot or tethering your phone to provide internet access for all your devices. This way, you can access maps, navigation apps, and useful travel resources even in areas with limited cellular coverage.

Before hitting the road, download offline maps of the areas you plan to explore. This precaution ensures that you can navigate without relying on continuous data coverage and helps you avoid unexpected data overage charges.

Make use of travel apps and websites to plan your itinerary, find nearby attractions, and discover local events. From restaurant reviews to real-time traffic updates, these apps offer a wealth of information at your fingertips, making your road trip experience more seamless and efficient.

To share your journey with friends and family, consider starting a travel blog or creating social media updates along the way. Sharing photos, stories, and experiences not only keeps your loved ones informed but also allows you to relive your adventure and connect with fellow travelers.

Traveling with others? Coordinate your plans and communicate effectively using messaging apps that work offline or over Wi-Fi. This ensures that everyone stays informed and connected throughout the trip, even in areas with limited cellular service.

Safety is paramount during your road trip, so ensure that you have a charged phone and a car charger on hand at all times. Having access to a charged phone can be crucial in case of emergencies or unexpected situations on the road.

With careful planning and the right resources, staying connected during your Atlanta road trip becomes a breeze. From access to maps and travel information to sharing your adventures with loved ones, staying connected enhances your journey and provides peace of mind throughout your exploration of Atlanta's highlights and hidden gems. Embrace the power of technology as your trusted travel companion, empowering you to make the most of your road trip adventure with confidence and ease.

10.3 Helpful Apps and Websites:

- Google Maps: A reliable navigation app that offers real-time traffic updates, turn-by-turn directions, and offline maps for areas with limited connectivity.

- Waze: A community-based navigation app that provides user-generated traffic and road information, helping you find the fastest routes and avoid delays.

- Maps.Me: Is an offline map app that allows you to download maps of specific regions, providing navigation without the need for constant data access.

- TripAdvisor: A comprehensive travel planning app that offers reviews, ratings, and recommendations for hotels, attractions, and restaurants in Atlanta.

- Roadtrippers: A road trip planning app that helps you create customized itineraries, discover unique attractions, and estimate travel times and distances.

- Yelp: Is a user-friendly app that provides reviews and ratings for local restaurants, bars, and attractions, helping you find the best spots for dining and entertainment.

- Event center: An app that lists local events and festivals, allowing you to discover cultural happenings and celebrations during your time in Atlanta.

- Meetup: An app that connects you with local groups and events based on your interests, providing opportunities to meet fellow travelers and like-minded individuals.

- The Weather Channel: An app that offers real-time weather forecasts, radar maps, and severe weather alerts to help you plan for varying weather conditions.

- Red Cross First Aid App: A comprehensive app that provides step-by-step instructions for handling common first aid emergencies, ensuring you are prepared for any health-related situations on your road trip.

- Google Translate: A powerful app that translates text and speech into multiple languages, bridging communication gaps and facilitating interactions with locals.

- Trail Wallet: A budget tracking app designed specifically for travelers, helping you monitor expenses and stay within your road trip budget.

By utilizing these helpful apps and websites, you can optimize your road trip experience, making it more seamless, efficient, and enjoyable. From navigating the city's streets to discovering local gems and preparing for various scenarios, these digital tools empower you to embrace the freedom of the open road with confidence and ease. Let these practical resources enhance your Atlanta road trip, ensuring that you make the most of your adventure and create lasting memories along the way.

Wrapping Up

As your road trip through Atlanta's captivating landscapes and cultural wonders draws to a close,This chapter is a poignant reflection on the journey you've undertaken, the memories you've made, and the lessons you've learned along the way. Wrapping Up is a heartfelt conclusion that invites you to savor the essence of your adventure and offers insights for future road trips.

11.1 Reflections on Your Journey

As you pause to reflect on your adventure, consider the moments that stirred your soul and left you in awe. Whether it was gazing at the city's iconic landmarks, savoring the flavors of local cuisine, or wandering through serene nature escapes, each experience has enriched your road trip with its unique essence.

Reflect on the connections forged along the way, the laughter shared with fellow travelers, the heartwarming encounters with locals, and the camaraderie formed during your journey. These connections have transformed strangers into friends and made the road a tapestry of shared experiences.

Contemplate the growth and self-discovery that occurred during your road trip. The open road has a way of revealing new aspects of ourselves, fostering resilience, and igniting a sense of wonder. Embrace the lessons learned and carry the spirit of exploration with you as you continue your journey beyond the road.

Consider the memories you've collected the snapshots of laughter, joy, and awe that now form a collage of your road trip experiences. Cherish these memories as treasures that will accompany you through life, enriching your spirit and reminding you of the beauty found in the pursuit of adventure.

In this moment of reflection, allow the road trip's tapestry of experiences to weave its way into your heart, leaving a mark that time cannot fade. Celebrate the beauty of exploration, the value of being present in the moment, and the transformative power of embracing the unknown.

As you bid farewell to Atlanta's highlights and hidden gems, know that the road continues to stretch before you, offering countless adventures yet to be written. May the reflections on your journey through Atlanta inspire you to embrace future road trips with an open heart and an insatiable curiosity. Let the road be your constant companion, guiding you to new horizons and evoking the magic of discovery wherever you may roam.

11.2 Tips for Future Road Trips

This section offers a treasure trove of practical tips and valuable insights to fuel your future road trip adventures beyond Atlanta. Drawing from the experiences and lessons learned during your journey, these tips empower you to plan, prepare, and embark on new road trip endeavors with confidence and enthusiasm:

- Embrace Flexibility:

Embrace the spontaneity and freedom that road trips offer. Embrace detours, unplanned stops, and unexpected discoveries along the way. Some of the most cherished moments arise from embracing the unforeseen.

- Plan Wisely But Not Too Much:

Strike a balance between planning your itinerary and leaving room for serendipity. Research the highlights and must-see destinations, but also allow yourself the freedom to veer off the beaten path and explore lesser-known treasures.

- Pack Smartly:

Pack essentials for comfort and safety, but keep it light. Remember to bring versatile clothing suitable for various weather conditions and activities. Minimize clutter to create a stress-free environment during your journey.

- Budget Thoughtfully:

Learn from your budgeting experiences in Atlanta, and apply those lessons to future road trips. Set a realistic budget, allocate resources wisely, and be prepared for unexpected expenses.

- Stay Connected:

Utilize technology to stay connected with loved ones and fellow travelers during your road trip. Sharing your experiences with others adds depth to your journey and fosters a sense of camaraderie.

- Embrace Local Culture:

Immerse yourself in the local culture and connect with the communities you visit. Engage with locals, try regional cuisine, attend cultural events, and embrace the diversity of each destination

- Capture Moments:

Take photographs, keep a travel journal, or start a travel blog to capture the essence of your road trip experiences. These memories will become cherished mementos of your adventures.

- Prioritize Safety:

Prioritize safety on the road. Ensure your vehicle is well-maintained, have a first aid kit on hand, and familiarize yourself with emergency resources along your route.

- Travel Responsibly:

Be mindful of the impact you have on the environment and the communities you visit. Travel responsibly, respecting local customs and natural surroundings.

- Embrace the Journey:

Remember that the road trip is not just about reaching destinations; it's about embracing the journey itself. Savor each moment, find joy in the simple pleasures, and cherish the connections made along the way.

As you embark on future road trips, let the experiences in Atlanta guide you, empowering you to create unforgettable memories and find wonder in every mile. Let each road trip be an opportunity to explore, learn, and grow, forging new paths with an adventurous spirit. The road awaits, and with these tips in mind, you are ready to craft more chapters in your road trip saga, filled with awe, discovery, and the joy of exploration

Conclusion

As we reach the final pages of "Travel Guide Road Trip to Atlanta: Embark on an Unforgettable Road trip to Atlanta's Hidden Gems," we find ourselves immersed in the magical tapestry of experiences woven throughout our journey. This travel guide has been more than just a collection of maps and itineraries; it has been a companion, guiding us through the heart of Atlanta's diverse highlights and captivating hidden gems.

From the bustling streets of downtown delights to the echoes of history found in historic landmarks, from the vibrant neighborhoods brimming with culture to the tranquil nature escapes that soothe the soul - we have explored the very soul of Atlanta, uncovering its many layers and facets.

Our road trip has been more than just a physical journey; it has been a voyage of self-discovery, connection, and awe. We have been touched by the kindness of locals, inspired by the art and music scene, and humbled by the beauty of the natural wonders that surround us.

Through the reader contributions and personal road trip experiences shared in these pages, we have been reminded of the power of travel to transform, uplift, and connect us all. The stories of serendipitous encounters, unexpected friendships, and profound insights are a testament to the magic that unfolds when we embrace the open road with an open heart.

As we conclude this road trip guide, let us carry the spirit of adventure and discovery within us, knowing that the joy of travel extends far beyond the final destination. Atlanta's hidden gems have become a part of our hearts, and the memories we have made will forever be etched in our souls.

May this guide continue to inspire and guide you on your own road trip adventures, not only in Atlanta but wherever the roads may lead you. As you embark on new journeys, may you embrace the beauty of exploration, the joy of the open road, and the profound connections that come from venturing into the unknown.

With gratitude for sharing this road trip to Atlanta's hidden gems, we bid farewell to this chapter and eagerly await the next adventure that awaits us. May the road continue to lead us to unforgettable moments, cherished memories, and the beauty that lies in every mile of our journey.

Printed in Great Britain
by Amazon

31746310R00056